KEEPING
BUSY

KEEPING BUSY

BUSY

NEW &
SELECTED
POEMS

ELSPETH SMITH

EYEWEAR PUBLISHING

First published in 2016
by Eyewear Publishing Ltd
74 Leith Mansions, Grantully Road
London w9 1LJ
United Kingdom

Typeset with graphic design by Edwin Smet
Author photograph (colour) by Annie Armitage
Author photograph (b/w) by Marriott's, Hastings, Sussex, taken June 1947,
St. Leonard's on Sea, Sussex - Elspeth aged 18.

Printed in England by TJ International Ltd, Padstow, Cornwall

ISBN 978-1-908998-92-7

*Eyewear wishes to thank Jonathan Wonham for his very generous patronage
of our press; as well as our other patrons and investors who wish to remain anonymous.*

WWW.EYEWEARPUBLISHING.COM

ELSPETH SMITH
was born in Ceylon in 1928
to British parents and spent her childhood
on a tea plantation. During the Second World War she
was sent to school in Edinburgh and then to St Leonards-
on-Sea, Sussex. She trained as a nurse before the NHS, and
then worked in hospitals across the country. In early middle
age she settled in Huddersfield, where she met
her husband, Allen, and qualified as a Health Visitor.
Her husband died twenty-five years after their marriage.
During her retirement, Smith began to seriously write
poetry. Her pamphlet *Wishbone* was published by
Smith/Doorstop (The Poetry Business).
Her debut collection, *Dangerous Cakes*, came
out from Eyewear in 2012,
to critical acclaim.

Elspeth Smith, June 1947

TABLE OF CONTENTS

🛎 DANGEROUS CAKES

● NEW POEMS

9

EDITOR'S INTRODUCTION

Writing a brief introduction to the work of a poet born in 1928
has its delights and unique challenges. Elspeth Smith, who began
writing seriously in the year 2000, and has kept busy ever since, is
a contemporary figure, yet we need to remind ourselves who else
was born in the 1920s: Edwin Morgan, Philip Larkin, Dannie Abse,
Elizabeth Jennings, Charles Tomlinson, U.A. Fanthorpe, Thom Gunn,
Peter Porter – Ted Hughes came along in 1930. Not that Smith writes
like any of them. Her poetry establishes its own mysteriously charming
world immediately, reminding readers of the poems of Walter de la
Mare, Stevie Smith, and Emily Dickinson.

These better-known poets may be her poetic precursors, though she
has no direct influences. Perhaps what she shares with other poets
of a deceptively modest, even light touch, is her gnomic, enigmatic
compression – her poems are some of the tiniest fables we have in the
English poetic tradition. The work is perfectly achieved for what it is,
without ever in the least appearing to try to be anything much. Hers is
some of the purest, most compelling, minimalist poetry I have ever read.
Elspeth Smith's sly poems limit themselves with obsessively-deployed
tropes – shoes, wine glasses, balloons, tea, cake, dancing, luggage,
schoolgirls – and then open up, somehow, into vast, mysterious places,
with a question or aperçu. It could be argued that Smith is a naïve
poet, in the sense that she appears not to have taken much account of
the more dramatic events in modern poetry, but this would be to miss
her genuine sense of form and image. Intentionally or not (and many
poets work under their own radars) she is an heir of the Imagists, the
Surrealists; and even has something of the whimsy of a Billy Collins.

Yet, her poetry is original, and all the more strangely inviting for that.
She has achieved what only the very best poets do – she has created a
way of making a poem that is now unmistakeably hers. It is possible to
read Elspeth Smith's poems repeatedly, and yet never find them yielding
all their secrets and implications, their horrors and delights. Just when
you think you have got the message, and can relax, you realise another
hidden depth charge is waiting for you.

At times, Elspeth Smith appears to be an optimist, aware of the gay and
silken pleasures of the days and nights; at other times, darkness and loss

is everywhere, a hairbreadth crack in the porcelain cup. Her vision is both light and dark, for curtains open and close. And, though her own life is, and was, doubtless filled with countless personal details of interest, she has pared all back in her poems, that, in their quiet universality, are all the more intimate, and devastatingly lovely.

This new paperback edition consists of her debut collection, *Dangerous Cakes*, which received support from an unusual mix of well-respected American and British poets, like Don Share, Alison Brackenbury and Lorraine Mariner – and a bonus that none of us could have hoped for – an even later flowering of creativity, begun in her mid-80s. As such, this is now a New & Selected, comprising a whole life's work, packed into about 15 years of compositional activity.

Readers hoping the many new poems gathered here are as good as some of the startling gems from her earlier Eyewear collection will not be disappointed – indeed, a handful are as good or better. Perhaps unsurprisingly, there are no major stylistic or thematic shifts – few other poets have created such a hermetic oeuvre, perfect in and of itself – and yet the new poems deepen, even still, some of the themes of a long day closing. Elspeth Smith has become England's leading poetic miniaturist, working with the smallest brushes on the smallest canvasses.

As I edited this new collection, it struck me how many echoes of 1940s songs are here – songs she might well have danced to as a younger girl: 'Dancing On The Ceiling'; '(Did You Ever Get) That Feeling In The Moonlight?'; 'Garden In The Rain'; 'I Had The Craziest Dream'; '(I'm Afraid) The Masquerade Is Over'; and 'I Hear Music' to name just a clutch. Not that is this sentimental poetry of a vintage, bygone era. Far from it. Smith's work collected here is powerfully concerned with key concerns for all readers, especially relevant now in a digital age: identity, ageing, memory, and what resists time to remain ours, when everything else in history, so-called nature, and the world is swept away. These poems, one hopes, one dreams, one feels, will last. They have a certain afterglow 11 that only the best poetry shares.

Todd Swift
Maida Vale, England
11 November, 2015

BY THE SAME AUTHOR

Wishbone
Dangerous Cakes

Dangerous Cakes

New Shoes

What will I do to you,
your lovely colour,
your unlined leather?
Will the agitation of my days
distort your shape?
Will my spoilt stampings,
disordered walking,
unbalanced running up and down
make marks on you?
Or will I fill you,
like champagne,
with all my little ecstasies,
make you dance?

Moment

The time was twilight.
Windows were clear,
blackout curtains discarded,
no coupons for new colours.
We could see the trees.
A piano was playing.

Not Talking

Where did you go
in the dark?
What do you hide
in your blank adult eyes?
What happened
when you went away
into the night?
Where have you been?
What have you seen?

Desk

Dragged from some attic,
covered with dust
in this clutter around us.
Bearing your name.

In Pencil

I am that lighter touch,
something more informal,
casual dress,
not suitable
to be officially presented
like those in print
or with that ink dark dignity.
I come in soft greys
or in harder lines.
Don't dispose of me
too soon.

On The Wall

Still blossoming.
Imprisoned
in your shabby frame.
Do you feel like
escaping?
To dance?
In some garden?
Stay in the picture
where you were painted.

That Room

The vague scent
of winter streets
clings to our coats.
We speak in whispers.
I am dreaming.

Nothing

Sometimes you come to me
in dreams.
You never speak.
I see you briefly.
And then
you are gone again.
It is nothing.
Why do I feel afraid?

Second Thoughts

We wait patiently
after the inspirations,
the wild ideas
have blown away.
That storm is over now.
Come to us
calmly.

Notice

Don't walk on me,
I can't take the weight
of your footsteps.
Only admire me,
smell my sweet green scent
as you come to this house
of heavy treasures.
I hear rumours.
Rumblings in flower beds.
Cows will not dare
to graze on me.
I will not be dug up.
Overcrowded towns
are not my problem.
Keep Off.

New Viewing

Wide-eyed windows,
eager to open.
That bell doesn't
ring anymore.
No switching on.
That light has gone,
wires cut or crossed.
All Electricity dead.
No longer
Highly Desirable.

Approaching

Why did I suddenly
pause
at the gate?
Why did I
tiptoe
up to the door?
Why did I tremble,
turning the key?
The place was empty.
Everything gone.
Only the roses were there
on the curtains.

Travel Talk

I like to travel to distant days,
can manage to fly as far away
as Nineteen Thirty Three
and hear the sound of crows.
I am frequently taken,
like so many others
to unforgettable Forty Five
with those sudden lights,
bonfires burning.
A favourite place is Fifty Six,
drenched in the scent
of the bluest grass.

Guest Room

I wait complacently.
My snowy sheets are smooth
beneath the feathered welcome.
My shelves are clear,
my cupboard space is winter clean.
No sounds of luggage up the stairs,
no madly beating feet,
no bursting suitcase
flinging me in disarray.

Next Morning

Nothing has changed,
everything is just the same.
No silver slipper on the stairs,
no left behind balloon
still wanting to keep dancing.

Written Clearly

You left a letter.
There is nothing to read between the lines,
no spaces to be eagerly filled.
Not one word stirring
in these neat phrases.
Sentences stand like sentries.
No hopeful drop of a comma,
no escaping exclamation,
no sudden wild italic.
Your last full stop is firm.

Fence

A little frill
around her flowers,
her strait-laced lawns,
the pathway waiting
for invited footsteps.
No sign of that intruder
coming quietly in the night.

Final Item

I am the last on the list.
A whole
meal for you tonight.
That knife is waiting.
I am ready to be cut,
devoured.

Handling

I place my hands in pure white gloves
to hide my bitten nails
rough skin
chipped polish

in rubber gloves
bubbles
rushing
through my fingers

in woollen gloves
saving
the desperation
of my winter day

in borrowed gloves
from sudden
other
hands.

Saved

I am a symbol of special elegance,
I am a reason for extra expense,
I am a delicate kiss on your lips.
I am the lap that is always ready,
the secret receiver of spilt cream.
I am the saviour of sticky fingers,
I am the colour of earth.
I am a flash of remembered fire,
I am a spark in the dark of your bag.
I am that table napkin
you almost crushed up in your hand.

Sweet Things

Keep away from those woods,
leave the trees with their secrets.
Come to these cut flowers,
cottage gardens,
little kittens in their collars
tripping through that painted gate.
A silver pot of tea,
neat slices of bread
these dangerous cakes.

No Tea Today

Cups
without any saucers.
Cups
on the floor.
Unwashed
in the sink,
leaves clinging desperately
to messages.
Cups needed immediately.
Cups
unavailable.

Trying It On

I come from sweet machinery,
lie smooth on every skin.
I dance in all the bubbles,
tumble joyfully around,
quite able
to be stretched.
Admittedly,
there is some whispering
amongst the purls and plains.
Ignore the woolly words,
'that sort
won't wear well.'

On The Moon

I come with balloons,
rattling crackers,
streamers to cover
the sky.
I am already
over the rainbow
but if I go too far
a special star
is well prepared
to shoot me
down to earth.

Bad Bargain

I hang unhappily,
my arms unwilling to open.
I am afraid of the rain,
those rough colours
that might be matched with me.
Take me back
to that scent of smooth carpets.
Say I'm unsuitable.
Say anything.

The Next People

Will the next people know
that the handles of my doors
must be rattled every night
until they almost break?
That my little taps and switches
have to be checked
again and again?
Will the next people know
that my window sills
and skirting boards
love to feel the dust
as it waits to settle
on whatever comes
to fill my empty spaces?

Miss Tiddy

moves in elevated places,
passes through garden party gates
we are not invited to enter.
Such sights
her discreet green eyes
have seen,
such mighty heights
she reaches,
such social trees
she climbs.
Our simple home
is understandably
not quite to her taste.
But we will

never

let anyone know

she was born in a barn.

Morning Coffee

This will be the last time
we sit here together,
you with your smooth hours of the day,
me with my sixty brittle minutes.
This will be the last time
I watch that creamy cup
raised smugly to your mouth,
see the delight in the icing
on every cake on the plate,
know there will be no difference
in the size of your waist,
the shape of your face.
This will be the last time
I listen to your indecisions
concerning your designer dresses,
smile politely at your escapades
with people in high places.
This will be the last time.
After you discover
what I have done.

Released

Such barking
in the jungle,
such mad miaowing,
such fluttering about.
We need our leads,
those hands
to stroke us.
We need carpets and cushions,
safe cages.
We can't relate
to wild lions and tigers,
will not consort
with common herds of buffaloes.

Captured

Tonight you will hear new music.
This place will change.
You will make unusual movements,
take strange steps,
speak unfamiliar words.
You came in innocence,
will stay forever
trapped in my pages.

Party

To you
inviting us wildly
into your place of rainbows

and you
spreading the table
with golden eggs

you
with your silver dreams
reaching your heaven

and you
from your midnight tent
in mysterious mountains

and you
from your sun and sky
and faraway stars

you
who were there
that night

Outbreak

The night has opened its arms again
spring singing.
Tight-lipped curtains
tear away from winter windows.
Panes are bare,
glass laughter cracked,
twilight all over the streets,
ready to face
the same old music.

Cutting The Grass

Someone is cutting the grass.
The air is scented.

I try to remember

a place,
a day

when someone was cutting the grass
and the air was scented.

With Care

Touch me gently.
I am everywhere around you.
I can be cut
exquisitely by diamonds,
stained with such colours.
Beware of me.
I can draw blood.

Scented

I touch your temples,
wrists,
whisper a secret
at your ear.
Linger,
letting everyone know
I was here.

Christening Spoon

So now you have found me.
I waited for you,
safely placed,
forgotten in the dance
of all your summer days.
Smell the dust on me.
See the stain on me.
Read your name on me.

Night Air

What does it bring
through your window?
Why do you smile
in your sleep?
What is this
strange
sense of excitement
tonight?

Gifts

Mine is the finest wine,
the sweetest cream,
the thickest soup,
the richest chicken,
the strongest coffee
for the silver stirring
of the night that has come at last.

Happy Ending

She is still sleeping.
Come
with your kiss.
Lead her peacefully
out of this world.

Evensong

Now you come nervously
kneeling here,
you who left me
long ago.
My bells still ring for you,
my candles burn.
Can my icy hands
reach out to you?
Can my fragile arms
manage to hold you
this time?
My music plays faintly.
Will you sing your song for me
once more?

Allowed Up

Footsteps
in strange places.
Walking
on swords.

Missing

I behaved beautifully.
Unseen,
unheard,
I left you.
Hands snatched me up
from the ground.
Efficient fingers
surround me now.
Brisk feet
could trip me away
to a thousand Safe Places.
Where are your arms?

Remembering

the waterfalls,
tea green bushes,
sea taking us
to what was called Home,
the excitement of snow.
Remembering black wartime nights,
a summer bursting with bewildered peace
on an earth that was new to us.
Remembering where footsteps took us,
eyes that were opened,
sometimes quickly closing again.
Remembering laughter.
Remembering the faces that came and went.
Coming, going.
Coming, going.
And all those days that blew away.

Cabin Trunk

Look at my labels,
you bright light luggage.
I sailed
down in that hold
under the sea.
You fly
up in the air
to the clouds.
We reached the same places.

Old Hats

Sweet sunbonnets
in flown away days.
Straw hats
fluttering flowers.
Hats at the tops
of those trees.
Mad Hats
making the most of it.
Sad solar topees
tossed to the sea.

School Train

The last time
we travelled together,
badges still on our breasts,
mottoes stuck to our hearts,
hats clinging to our heads

we remembered the first time.

Afternoon Tea

In this cup
I see the leaves
of long ago
from hillsides
of lost places.

Entering

The door has opened easily.
I am becoming quite efficient,
learn quickly.
This room is beautiful.
My dirty fingers
stroke the curtains,
I cross the carpet,
my steps are soft.
Why am I here?

Tea Alone

The stirring of a silver spoon again.
The blooming of blue moons.
The silly stirring
of the silver spoon.

The stirring of a silver spoon.
A message coming soon.
The shaky stirring
of the silver spoon.

The stirring of a silver spoon.
The feelings of a fool.
That incessant stirring
of the silver spoon.

Theatre Seat

Each night
I fold another body in my arms.
They come to me
eagerly,
barely aware of the part I play.
Now they have gone,
the curtains are closed.
I am empty,
vacant,
waiting for the next performance.

Until Next Year

Dropped blossoms on the stage
lie waiting to be swept away.
The crowd moves smoothly
filled with the cream of the evening.
Out in the street
a balloon floats by
to the sea
in the rain.

Autumn Ball

It is morning
in my garden.
All night
I listened
to the wind.
Those golden skirts
hang tattered.
You have danced too long.

A Strange Time

Something strange is happening
in the woods,
in the wind.
Something strange is happening
in the lights,
in the rain.
Something strange is happening
to us
again.

Flu Jabs

See us
this morning
filling the street.
Girls who waited
to be asked to dance.
Boys who nervously
crossed the floor.
Ready for the waltz
into a world of bluebirds.

Shoe Box

Did you hold some strong brogues
for walks together?
Or soft soles that paced the floors
to wild cries in the night?
Sudden stilettos
in rustling paper?
Little hushed puppies
for well trained steps?
A pair to slip on
and on till the end?
What do I do with letters
one is expected to read?
And who is this face
I can't quite place?

Drinks

Will it be tinkling crystal tonight
or a plastic cup to hold your cold water,
exotic cocktails at your lips,
champagne again with more applause?
Is this the hour
of the herbal infusion,
sips of sweet tea,
some nice kind milk?
Just a draught of good juice
from the fruits of the earth?
Always another alternative,
that vicious liquid standing by.

Ringing Off

A telephone rings round a room.
The gentle beige on the vacant walls,
the staring space on the carpet.
The stain that never went away,
the window without the sparkles
missing the warmth of those curtains.
The sound is spreading up the stairs.
But the dreams have gone,
there is nothing there.
A telephone rings round an empty room,
saying goodbye.

Doorbell

The sound comes softly,
from nervous fingers at times
or impatiently repeated.
Even with a little thrill.

Very occasionally
in the night,
just the slightest touch.
Then it has gone.

Lost

Where are the trees tonight?
Where are the houses?
Where is the church?
Where is the school?
Why is there only
the moon
and the snow?

Harrogate

'Shall we walk across The Stray?'
they say.
But I prefer
to see that washing line
still stretching high
above the grass.

Nailed to the garden gate,
the notice we insisted on
states
'No Admittance.'

Revisit

'He is still here,
she is still here,
the garden is blooming.
But I remember a child.
A beautiful child.
Tell me,
where is the child?'

'I am the child.'

Cancelled

Dawn will not break.
Morning will not come at your call.
The afternoon is lost.
Evening is sleeping.
A page in that diary will be empty,
a space on the calendar is blank.
This day will not take place.

Last Meal

Music was subdued
the mood had changed.
Still those scents.
Delicious spices on the
Dish of Summer Evening.
An icy touch
of sparkling water
on those smiling lips.
No wine
on our table for two.

Scene

This is the hour
of the morning.
This is the month
of the summer.
This is the day
of the week.
These are the sounds
in the trees.
This is the dress
I was wearing.

Red

Now I am Red.
I am that Red Letter,
I am those Red Shoes,
I am Scarlett O'Hara,
I am Red Riding Hood.
I am Red,
I am Red.

Little Lost Property

You must have been dancing.
Is it a secret?
You must have been part of the charm
of some belle of the ball.
You must have been
a bit of fun.
You must have been dancing
that night.

Wine Glass

This is not
how I expect to find you.
You should be sparkling
in the morning sun
fresh from a bowl of bubbles.
Ready to be lightly touched
by soft selective lips.
Not with these empty others
on the floor.

Saviour

What would you do
without me
driving you
so delightfully
to Drink?

Changing Day

Flip flop sandals
flap their way
along hot pavements.

A high pair of heels
steps daintily
through puddles.

Little silver slippers
trip out
into the evening.

Bare feet
are beginning to dance.

Clear Glass

I gave you the jam
for your bread,
water for your wild flowers.
Let me go grandly,
crashing in a million
glittering splinters
with vessels
that held wine.

Eating Place

The cakes never came.

We wanted plates
ready to break for us,
spoons to stir,
cups to hold.

The tea was cold.

Salad

What language will you speak
to me tonight?
Which of those words
I do not understand
will whisper
of the green that has gone,
the taste of the days
that were left behind?

You Were

the permanent audience not always
applauding enough,
the backdrop behind every drama,
the lines I forgot,
the song I couldn't always sing,
the intervals between the scenes,
the makeup saving my face,
the wings where I stood protected,
the dressing room ready for my return,
the Gallery that was packed,
the Box that was empty,
the House I occasionally brought down,
the flowers that came at last,
the curtain falling.

Another Year

January is a bit of glitter
lying with the litter in the street.
January is snow
covering the rubbish.
January is a cold
hot water bottle.

February is a young heart
beating slightly faster.
February is the song
you are singing again.
February is a Valentine
from the wrong person.

March is a fine
line of daffodils
between winter and spring.
March is a wild idea,
an office argument,
a slight scandal.

April is grass growing green.
April is an opening umbrella.
April is a little lamb
dancing while it has the chance.

April is a shop window
crammed with chocolates.
May is a world
of blossoms at your feet,
a summer frock,
a slimmer salad,
a daring step
in a fresh direction.

June is a clock
in a silent hall,
a frenzied pen,
a last party.
June is a fleet
of ships in the night.

July is a packed Departure lounge,
a queue of cars to the coast.
July is one more slug in the garden.
Mud on the carpet,
a new novel.
July is moonlight.

August is luggage
at hotel doors,
a sea of sheets
on corridors.
August is a summer kiss
goodbye.

September is sun sparkling.
September is a stretch of polished floors,
a page turning,
a pile of clean clothes.
Spilt milk,
strong coffee.

October is a kitten
playing with a golden leaf.
October is a woollen scarf,
an evening class.
October is a broomstick
sweeping away the days.

November is a lit building
on a dark afternoon,
a display of diamond rings
for eager fingers,
a silver shoe
on a wet pavement.

December is a fire
crackling with cheer,
every spirit of Christmas
invited with desperate arms.
December is a star
still shining.

Misadventure

That was the wish that should not have been made.
That was the dream that should not have been dreamed.
That was the music that should not have played.

That was the road that should not have been crossed.
Those were the stairs that should not have been
climbed.
That was the wish that should not have been made.

That was the match that should not have been struck.
That was the flame that should never have danced.
That was the music that should not have played.

This is the stitch that should not have been sewed.
This is the needle that should not have pricked.
This is the wish that should not have been made.

This is the cake that should not have been cut.
This is the flower that should not have been plucked.
This is the music that should not have been played.

That was the tale that should not have been told.
That was the secret that no one should know.
That was the wish that should not have been made.
This is the music that should not have played.

Slipping Out

I leave you
with the last
of my laughter.
An untouched glass
still sparkling.

Wishbone

The feast is over.
I am stripped and shining
after the wildest night.
I watched the wine flow,
balloons rise to the roof,
saw the great star
at the top of the tree,
felt every piece of flesh picked from me
as it must be.
I hold a privileged position.
In my little brilliance
your fingers take me up.
Your words are secrets in the sky.
Now I am high in your hands.

Wait.

Your wish will come true.

Fancy Dress

Will you come as Spring,
all teasing green,
tripping in sweetly
on tiptoeing feet?
Appear as Winter,
freezing white,
icicles dropping
from silver fingers?
Would you be Summer,
smothered red,
an invitation
to a bed of roses?
Or risk arriving
undisguised?

Morning Dormitory

Six neat beds,
counterpanes straightened
like narrow paths
for us to tread.
Six towels
hanging damply
after the freezing strip wash.
Six flannels
wet from faces
craving make up.
Six pairs of slippers
belonging to feet
eager for
vague
wild dancing.

Lights Out

Follow the crocodile of ghosts
to the top of vanished stairs
where the sleeping girls are dreaming
of the kiss that will rudely awaken them.
Go to the overgrown garden,
hear old sounds of tennis balls.
Listen to forbidden whispers
in the night's nine o'clock silence.
Chestnut trees are spreading over
small gym-knickered figures
hanging dutifully upside down,
all in the cause of learning
to be strictly civilized.
Little lost conduct stars
laugh in the grass.

After the fire.

Retreating

I packed my blackest bag.
A fresh brush for my clenched teeth,
a sponge still holding little drops
from familiar taps,
a box of chocolates
for the hungry nights ahead.
Unscented soap
clung smugly to the basin.
Towels were waiting
to dry me up
after my sins were washed away
in all those quantities of hot and cold
wildly running water.
How many was I expected to have
committed?
I slipped downstairs.
Escaped again.

Cutting Up

Now I am closed eyes,
folded hands,
carefully controlled.
I followed pretty patterns,
prepared the way for every stitch,
all those little needles
ran smoothly through the paths I made.
Then my blades began to tremble.
I was tearing at the paper,
slashing at the letters.
I started on the sheets,
the shirts,
the curtains.

I was taken away
with the other sharp possessions.

Glimpse

Leaves concealed it,
thick green summer
keeping the secrets.

Stark branches
bare the truth.

Soon snow will be falling.

Teddy Bear

Your ears have never heard
those words of love.
Your eyes have never seen
this bright white bedroom.
Your mouth will not move
from where it's stitched.
Secrets are safe with you.

Same Age

You must play with others of your own age.
Enjoy your toys together,
make a joyful noise together,
hit each other on your little heads.

You must stick with others of your own age.
Explore the world together,
lead each other
into every way to go astray.

You must stay with others of your own age.
Sit and stare together,
at the empty spaces of the day,
prepare to rest in peace together.

Madsummer

Sun is let loose now.
Days dance crazily,
screaming green.
Sky is higher,
bursting blue.
Flowers bloom outrageously
like uncontrolled laughter.
Feet slip from sandals
onto burning ground.

This Window

Shows you the tops of those trees,
brings you the sound of those birds,
gives you the warmth from that sun,
the light from that moon.
This window
with bars.

Statues

Are you waiting
for the music
that suddenly stopped
as you danced
in your garden?

Leg

Waiting for the flames,
a length of skin and bone,
chewed playfully
by some mischievous malignancy.
An elegant shape, death white,
once wild high kicking Can Can black
dizzily fish netted,
catching every necessary eye.
Pale nails, no longer painted,
on toes that tripped
through tempting places.
> That dancing foot
> will bravely take
> this step alone.

Idle Hand

Whose number can I tap tonight?
Who dare I disturb?
Whose turn is it
to suffer?
What can I offer?

I have a little scandal...

Meeting You

I know these eyes
but not these grinning
sticks of teeth,
these hands stretched out to me
like frantic branches.
A winter tree,
how had you danced that summer?

I know these eyes.
They stare at me
from every mirror.

Bad Luck

I sparkled
at all you were told
in the sweet heat
of those odd moments.
My broken bits will bring you the next
seven years.

Going Down

Now I belong to diamonds
Oh Elizabeth,
what have you done?
Taking me to all these
heaven-scented, cherished memories,
the red door, the sunflowers, the blue grass?
I splash ecstatically,
I am high
flying,
dabbing, drenching, spraying,
playing a game,
hoping I can pay the price.

I go down
to the safe waters of lavender.

Handshake

Will these fingers keep meeting?
Will something pass
occasionally
between them?
Will they quite cheerfully
wave themselves away?
Will they blow kisses?
Dry tears?
Stroke softly?
Never touch again?

New Arrival

Wait.
It is not yet time to take me
as you took those others,
in your stride.
I am still a closed curtain.
An unopened envelope,
my writing not known to you.
Your folded paper
showing that odd inviting word.
A soft slice of bread
ready for toasting.
Will you fill me
with all your overflowing
or only ignore me,
letting me waste away?
Will I be welcomed,
cherished,
remembered forever?

A Promise

I am here at last
surrounded by roses,
touching the glass of your window.
I peer
into an empty room.

Last Invitation

Come.
I am covered with flowers,
exquisitely polished,
ready to perish
in fire or earth.
Come to me breathlessly.
Need nothing more.

Outside

Here is the gate,
waiting.
Here is the open door,
the windows
sparkling.
This is the house
I must never enter.
This is the bell
I must never ring.

New Poems

Response

A cool drink,
smooth soup.
Crusty bread
gently broken.
Salad,
neat and green.
A sudden tangy
touch of spice,
not known before.

Out In The Grass

Your blood is pounding
with the music from hooves,
the drumming of the running
round and round.
That quick flick
of a disciplined whip.
Dance for us now.

Meeting

Immediately
about it.
Taking it gently,
considering it carefully,
discussing it calmly,
seeing another side.
Getting to grips with it,
right to the root of it,
the very bottom of it.
Leaving it alone.
Walking away from it,
letting it sort itself out.
Coming back to it.

Bridge

The river
is about
to break its banks.
Trees
are losing their leaves.
Soon
these footsteps
will be crossing me.

In The Shed

Brushes and brooms
that swept the dust
from shoes that went away
to different lives.
A table with
no places set
where no more
cards are laid.
A baby's cot
no longer rocked
by hands
now ruling other worlds.

End Of The Month

Every day
is dancing through the week.
At times
they come slowly
past difficult minutes
or wildly
round hour after hour,
almost forgetting
their names and their dates.
Now dancing again
before slipping away.

Procession

Now the cows come.
Moving smoothly,
chorus girls,
a corps de ballet,
nuns in prayer.
Prepared
for presentation.
Complacently
to Market.

Something Burning

Is it the trees,
those forests again?
Is it a kettle
without enough water,
a letter of love,
an oven too high,
a fire
with children
dancing round?
Is it that smoke,
as of old,
in your eyes?

Keeping Busy

Making
a song and dance,
raising the roof,
stirring all the tiny storms
in every teacup.
Making
a fuss,
excuses,
amends,
new friends,
mad plans.
Making
the mind up,
the face up.
A sudden decision.
The most of it,
a mess of it,
the best of it.
Just a little more hay
while the sun is still shining.

Eiderdown

Tonight I share your sleep again,
with you in your dreams
once more.
Now in this empty house
on this bare floor.
Tomorrow you will tip me
neatly away
with the rest
and go.

Wanting To Talk

I speak with my eyes,
my hands,
my agitating,
tightly gripping,
pleading
fingers.

Place Of Declaration

These envelopes are empty.
The lines behind
those Bonds of Basildon
not needed now.
You are off to wild websites,
dancing with the dots and coms.
There is nothing
but the spoken word.

Old Song

You have been at
that hemlock again.
Your heart is aching,
still under the spell
of some nightingale
who sang to you of summer.

Same Table

The wildest rice
tonight.
Poppadoms scatter
slightly madly.
A reckless dip
into a dish of spices.
That first daring taste
to be taken again.

Lifetimes

The first time,
the good time,
the short time,
the sad time,
the fine time,
the high time,
the last time,
the long time.
That one time.

Tray

Today I bear
two cups and saucers
carefully
upstairs.
In the kitchen
teaspoons whisper,
knives stand sharply,
forks prepare
to have that other stab.
Such steaming,
sizzling,
such wild stir frying.
No free and easy
finger food on me tonight.

Permanent Student

Preparing
to make
the biggest mistake
of my life.
And learn
the next lesson.

Whatever

Will it be daffodils
some time in Spring
or summer roses?
Perhaps Autumn leaves,
should they be falling.
Or will it be holly

laid out in display?

In Hiding

In this scarlet darkness
I am a secret thing,
asleep in sweet green bones.
Almost too tender
to hold me tight.
I will be the candle
on your birthday cake,
too difficult to blow.
The paint stain
on your party dress.
A Christmas parcel
holding another unwanted toy.

View

I saw the path
where I was never lead,
roses that I never gathered,
hay I never helped to make,
ignoring the sun that had come.
I only saw one swallow,
there should have been more.
I never tried to take a taste
of that forbidden fruit
or go over to the other side
and check the colour of the grass.
I saw them all
from where I sat.

On Show

See how I blossom
in beautiful gardens.
In the best crystal vases,
exquisite arrangements
with ribbons,
sweet leaves.
See how I blossom
at windows.
Watch me grow thorns.

Perhaps With Candles

Flowers,
a silver
glitter.

Shadows,
folded hands,
unspoken words.

Flickering
lights,
in winter rooms.

Appointment

I am waiting to see
you who will know
the secrets
of my beating heart,
the breaths I take,
those feelings in my bones.
I bring you my body.

Finding The Words

With a flourish of a feather,
a dip into a well.
With a great display,
from some showering fountain.
With a bright little ball
pointing it out.
With a net
that has captured the world.

First Appearance

Some day you may,
who knows,
hold some great
eminent position
on this place
of corridors and flowers,
smoothly moving trolleys,
busy little drips,
helping to keep hearts beating.
Where now you make your entrance,
completely naked.

Now Ripe

Rosy and ready
too eager
to leave your tree.
Only careful hands
should pluck you.
You shall be
the sweetest fruit,
picked for
the sweetest salad.
Apple
of that eye.

Streets

Where feet
Once
Wanted to dance.

Little Village

A slight sunset,
no mad magic
in the sky.
I am a stranger.

Hidden Silver

I should be stirring
sugar lumps
in some elegant
afternoon tea.
Books and papers
smother me.
A ball point pen
is rushing round
that cold
cup of coffee.

Ankles

We take our steps
in simple strides,
hearty marches,
Scottish reels,
Irish jigs.
A silly wish
at times
for little bells
to ring around us.

Down On The Desk

All is in order.
Every file and folder
in just the right place.
I start to sparkle.
Flash.
Switch on and off.
I shine
on strange writing,
wild words.
Dream now
in darkness.

Brushing Off

I have played my part,
left you with that
little touch
of colour in the corner.
A splash of happiness,
the picture is painted.

Head Of Hair

We grew together.
Flew freely,
no tying back,
no twisted pigtails,
no tearing,
pulling.
Sometimes a little thrill
from teasing fingers
running through.
Nothing to harm us.
Until those scissors came.

Just Arrived

In a difficult position,
an awkward situation,
a sorry state.
A fever,
a dream.
Under a cloud,
an impression,
illusion.
Up the wrong tree.
On a whim,
on a high.

Only Once

Afternoon.
No evening dress,
no bacon and eggs
at dawn.
But my hand
was dabbling
in the water.

The Last Glass

Amongst the burst balloons
Torn paper hats
Snapped crackers
Silver spoons
Stained in their saucers
The party is not over.

Pink Paint

This is my colour tonight.
All day
I gently stroked those walls
Slipped smoothly
Through the other rooms
My bristles are thick
With sweetness.

Taking You Back

Now he lets you out
to wander through the ruins
of that life you knew.
Those flames have raged
like red correcting pencils.
Is this a bit
of the library floor?
Could this glass
be a part
of our dormitory window?
He lets you in again
from a place he can never enter.

The Neatness Tea

A teapot
on a table
holding tea.

A dormitory
kept tidy
for certain
stipulated weeks.

No chipped enamel
jugs for us
in the gym
that day.

Allocated packets
of strictly rationed butter
for bread with
cheese.

Gym Mistress

Those eager legs
were ready
to pedal down the hill.
The war was over,
term was new,
chestnut trees
like life,
in bloom.
Just too late.
The train had left.
Soon
perhaps,
another
attempt at escape.

Half-Term Party

The night we blossomed
in parachute silk
or simply
in Utility,
tasting a little
permitted lipstick
on excited smiles.
The night we danced
the Conga
through the Dining Room,
the corridors.
The night we went wild.

Rhododendron Garden

This was a sacred place.
No outdoor shoes,
no little extra
tap or ballet steps.
Just that
once a summer day
of Nightingales,
Pipes of Pan,
Romeos and Juliets,
Twelfth Nights and Tempests.
Now
remember it.

Good Fairy

My borrowed basket
from Red Riding Hood
holds a wand I cannot wave,
wishes I can't grant.
These silly Cinderella feet
will never fit the shoes
I volunteered to wear.
I tumbled down
too many hills
with my overflowing
pails of water.
I dare not spread my busy wings
in this strange place
of tempting plates
and empty beds.

All Right

I have left you too long.
Wild statements
banked high.
Orders
who don't know how you stand.
A threatening letter
mixed up with sticky labels.
I am coming.
You shall take your rightful places
in the drawers of my desk.

Luggage

Was the decision
made too quickly?
Are you the right shoes?
Are you the most suitable suit?
Will they be warm enough?
Will we come to dark cupboards,
some strange chest of drawers?
Or find ourselves
flung in a heap,
back on that bed?

Wrong Road

Eyebrows raise
with anxious questions,
eyes express desire
to be of assistance,
lips smile kindly,
eager hands gesticulate.
Fresh coffee
sends inviting scents
across the street.
Signposts stand by.
Nobody knows
I am running away.

Plates

Ready with offerings.
Little legs
that ran their races.
Shoulders
having known
the feel of tears
along the way.
Wings now still.
Breasts
laid bare for you.

Drawing Room

I will not be called Lounge.
Let the music
from those silver spoons
play in me again.
I have lost the sparkle
of my chandeliers,
my windows are stripped
of rich curtains.
Bring me Mahogany,
place great paintings
on my walls.
I knew stiff lips,
blood that was blue.
Let me cling
to my name.

Seeing My Sights

I should be
in and out of temples,
up and down mountains,
dashing through jungles,
on and off great elephants.
I stay
mesmerised
by red brick sunset
on white four walls.

Planned Journey

I go slowly down the street,
studying numbers.
Two big black digits
suddenly
jump out at me.
It is afternoon.
A quiet time.
I wait.
Watching those windows.

Gates

Now we are closed
to you.
Not time
yet
for any celebration,
We will be waiting,
painted in gold,
decorated with pearls.

Shopping

These windows bewitch me.
My morning stars,
my hunting ground,
nourishment.
My lunch and breakfast,
little elevenses,
a scent of flowers.
This is the grass
that is always green,
that open space I crave,
the closed doors
at a time for other worship.

Pigeons

Where are the words
that could have been fastened
to our little feet?
High on our listed buildings,
we hear the stories
cooed to us.
Communications,
copper plated,
photographed messages,
heavily censored.
Delicate pages,
light as air.
Emails passing us by.

In Darkness

I drive through the night
to an unknown place,
trees on either side of me.
No sound of any human voice.
Only the wind
outside my bedroom window.

No Rings

on these fingers.
Hands can flutter freely,
wrists can twist handles,
knuckles knock on all the doors,
nails tap mischievously
on windows.
Palms stretch out.
Upturned.
Exposed.

Cactus

This prickly present
surrounded
by sweets and scents
on this morning
of her Happy Day.
You are part
of her dream
of unseen sunsets,
stars.
Take her there
with you
tonight.

Nightgown

She sees it from her window
as she sits here,
free at last
to dream all day.
It is hanging on the line
with all the others.
The colour is white,
like a christening robe,
a party frock,
that wedding dress
she almost wore,
those frilly
hidden bits and pieces.
She asks if she might wear it
on the day she goes away.

Governess

Step out
From your Victorian novel
Into some future world
For a better position
As a celebrity girl.

Masked

But we still
See those eyes
Telling
The truth.

On The River

Still rushing through
The slightly muddy
Colours of the past.

Now
In the pink present

Already,
A glimpse
Of blue future.

As we go
Flowing away.

Not Necessary

I am flinging it out,
it is wasting
my space.

Taking
all the room I need.

Flinging it out.

Bringing it back.

Good New Year

Take it gently.
Its little days
are not quite used to you.
Christmas cards
still linger.
That children's party,
some grand ball.
These minutes move quickly.
Hours fly open.
The weeks are vacant,
icy clean.

Acknowledgements

A few of these poems first appeared in the Smith/Doorstop pamphlet *Wishbone* (The Poetry Business, 2007); and in *The North* and *Poetry Northeast* (USA).

Grateful acknowledgement is expressed here to the editors and publishers. My most grateful thanks to Todd Swift for all his help and encouragement and to the Eyewear team. Thanks also to Edwin Smet for his very impressive design of my Eyewear books.

◯◯ EYEWEAR PUBLISHING

SQUINT

BRIEF BOOKS FOR A BUSY WORLD
Look More Closely